D1095944

A Robbie Reader

Johnny Gruelle

AND THE STORY OF
RAGGEDY ANN AND ANDY

Josepha Sherman

Mitchell Lane
PUBLISHERS

P.O. Box 196
Hockessin, Delaware 19707
Visit us on the web: www.mitchelllane.com
Comments? email us: mitchelllane@mitchelllane.com

Printing   1   2   3   4   5   6   7   8

A Robbie Reader

Albert Einstein	Alex Rodriguez	Charles Schulz
Dale Earnhardt Jr.	Donovan McNabb	Dr. Seuss
Henry Ford	Hilary Duff	Jamie Lynn Spears
Johnny Gruelle	LeBron James	Mia Hamm
Philo T. Farnsworth	Robert Goddard	Shaquille O'Neal
The Story of Harley-Davidson	Syd Hoff	Thomas Edison
Tony Hawk		

Library of Congress Cataloging-in-Publication Data
Sherman, Josepha.
    Johnny Gruelle and the Story of Raggedy Ann and Andy / by Josepha Sherman.
        p. cm. — (A Robbie reader)
    Includes bibliographical references and index.
    ISBN 1-58415-359-8 (lib. bdg.)
    1. Gruelle, Johnny, 1880?–1938—Juvenile literature. 2. Illustrators—United States—Biography—Juvenile literature. 3. Authors, American—20th century—Biography—Juvenile literature. 4. Children's stories—Authorship—Juvenile literature. I. Title. II. Series.
NC975.5.G776S54 2005
741.6'42'092—dc22

                                                                    2005004251

ABOUT THE AUTHOR: Josepha Sherman is a prolific author with more than 60 books in print. The owner of Sherman Editorial Services, Josepha has also written a six book series on alternative energy (Capstone); *The History of the Internet* (Franklin Watts); *Bill Gates: Computer King* (Millbrook); and *Dale Earnhardt Jr.* and *The Story of Harley-Davidson* (both for Mitchell Lane Publishers). In addition, she is a native New Yorker, has a degree in archaeology, loves to tinker with computers, and follows the NY Mets.

NOTE: The names and depictions of Raggedy Ann and Raggedy Andy are trademarks of Simon & Schuster.

PHOTO CREDITS: All photos are courtesy of Tom and Joni Gruelle Wannamaker, Patricia Hall, and the Raggedy Ann and Andy Museum.

ACKNOWLEDGMENTS: The following story has been thoroughly researched, and to the best of our knowledge and represents a true story. While every possible effort has been made to ensure accuracy, the publisher will not assume liability for damages caused by inaccuracies in the data. The author and Mitchell Lane Publishers would like to thank Tom and Joni Gruelle Wannamaker and Patricia Hall for their cooperation and assistance with this book.

TABLE OF CONTENTS

Chapter One
The Contest...5

Chapter Two
Beginnings 9

Chapter Three
Mr. Twee Deedle 13

Chapter Four
Raggedy Ann 19

Chapter Five
Raggedy Ann and Andy Live On......................23

Selected Works...28
Chronology 29
Glossary 30
To Find Out More..31
Index 32

This is a picture of Johnny in 1918. He was thirty-eight when the picture was taken.

The Contest

Johnny Gruelle and his brother, Justin, were hiking through the woods of Connecticut. It was a chilly autumn day, and the trees were beginning to lose their leaves. The two brothers were grown up. They were catching up on old times when they heard the hooting call of a horn. It was the horn their mother blew when she wanted them to hurry home. Johnny and Justin stared at each other. Then they dashed back to the Gruelle farmhouse. What had happened?

It was nearly dark by the time they got to their mother's home. As they rushed up the front steps, breathless from their run, they found their mother waiting on the porch. She

This is Johnny's portrait of Mark Twain. Mark Twain was the **pseudonym** (SUE-duh-nim), or fake name, of Samuel Clemens. He is one of the most famous American authors.

Johnny also drew political (puh-LIT-ih-kuhl) cartoons. A political cartoon makes fun of items in the news. This cartoon shows a man standing for Big Business being stopped by a rock standing for labor, or the everyday workers.

THE STUMBLING BLOCK

waved a letter at them. It was for Johnny, and it was from a New York City newspaper, the *New York Herald.*

Some time before, Johnny had entered a cartooning contest that the newspaper was running. The contest, he'd thought, would decide whether or not he had any real talent as a **cartoonist**. Now the answer was here.

Johnny tore open the envelope and read the letter. He grinned.

"I'm going to New York!" he cried. "The editors at the *New York Herald* want to meet me!"

He didn't yet know why. The letter didn't tell him very much. But if the editors wanted to see him, it could only be good news.

Johnny Gruelle was already a professional cartoonist—but maybe now he would be a famous one.

Johnny and his wife, Myrtle, stand in front of their house. This was their home in Florida.

Beginnings

Richard Buckner Gruelle of Arcola, Illinois, was a happy man in 1880. True, he and his wife, Alice, had very little money. He was an artist, and artists didn't earn very much. But Richard and his wife loved each other. They were looking forward to the birth of their first child. On December 24, 1880, a baby boy was born. He was named John Barton Gruelle. He would be called Johnny.

When Johnny was still very young, his family moved to Indianapolis (Indee-uh-NAP-uh-lus), Indiana. Johnny and his younger brother and sister, Justin and Prudence, grew up surrounded by artists and writers. Soon Johnny was drawing his own **cartoons**. He began carrying a pencil and paper around with him wherever he went. Instead of becoming a painter like his father, Johnny continued drawing cartoons.

When he was in his late teens, Johnny worked as an artist for several of the local newspapers. By the time he was nineteen, he knew he wanted to earn his living as an artist. He also fell in love with a young lady named Myrtle (MUR-tel) Swann.

On March 23, 1901, Johnny and Myrtle married. By the middle of 1902, they were the parents of a little girl, Marcella. Now Johnny had a family to support. In 1903, he became the assistant illustrator for a newspaper called the *Indianapolis Star.* Then he was offered a better job as sports cartoonist for *The Cleveland Press.* Johnny, Myrtle, and little Marcella moved to Cleveland.

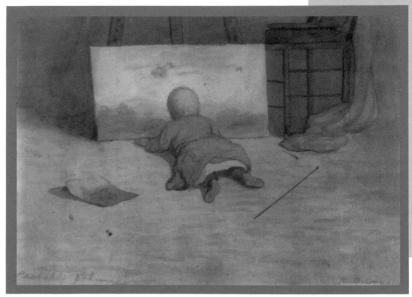

This painting was made by Johnny's father, Richard. It is probably a painting of Johnny when he was a baby. It just goes to show that being an artist must run in the family.

This is Marcella in 1904. She is busy playing. Maybe she didn't even know her picture was being taken.

Here is an original page from the *New York Herald*. It shows a full page of cartoons about Mr. Twee Deedle. He is giving his human friends some magic fun.

Mr. Twee Deedle

Johnny might have stayed a sports cartoonist in Cleveland. But in 1910, his parents moved to Connecticut. When Johnny and Myrtle visited them, they liked the area so much that they moved there, too.

That year, Johnny heard about the contest being held by the *New York Herald.* Prizes would be awarded for the best cartoons. There wasn't much time left in which to enter. Johnny worked through the night, drawing two cartoons. He entered them both. "I did not really expect to get the prize," he said, "but I thought I would see what I could do."

To his complete surprise, Johnny won both first and second prize. The first-prize winner was a drawing of a funny little fairy, Mr. Twee Deedle. The editors at the newspaper liked that character so much that they gave Johnny a contract. It was for a **continuing comic strip** about Mr. Twee Deedle. The editors said about Johnny, "Children will recognize at once that they have . . . a new friend . . . who knows what children like."

Johnny wrote and drew many stories about Mr. Twee Deedle. He also sent stories and drawings to other newspapers and magazines, such as *McCall's* and *The Ladies' World.*

Around this time, Johnny had visited his parents. In the attic he found a rag doll that belonged to his grandmother. He painted a face on the old doll and named it Raggedy Ann. He gave it to his daughter, Marcella. She loved Raggedy Ann. In some of his cartoons, Johnny drew the doll, usually being dragged behind a child.

Then sadness struck in November 1915. Marcella, barely thirteen, had suffered all her

Marcella with her dog "Rags." She looks like she's dancing with him. Behind them is her doll carriage.

life from **valvular** heart disease. In that year she was **vaccinated** (VAX-in-ayted) for smallpox. A vaccination is a shot that prevents disease. Today, vaccinations are safe and ordinary. But in 1915, mistakes could be made, and a second vaccination was given to Marcella. She fell ill from an unsterile (un-STER-ihl) needle. Even though she was under a doctor's care and got plenty of bed rest, she died.

Johnny kept Marcella's spirit alive by naming one of his storybook characters after her. In the introduction to his book the *Raggedy Ann Stories* he says that Marcella was the one that found the rag doll in the attic instead of him. And in 1929, Johnny named an entire book of tales after Marcella.

Johnny named this book after his daughter, Marcella. She was a character in some of his Raggedy Ann and Andy stories. Sadly, he wrote this one after her death. It was written in honor of her.

In the book, Marcella does things with Raggedy Ann and friends, such as have tea parties. Johnny drew a very pretty Marcella. She does look like the real Marcella grown up a little.

DESIGN.

J. B. GRUELLE.
DOLL.
APPLICATION FILED MAY 28, 1915.

47,789.

Patented Sept. 7, 1915.

Fig. 2.

Fig. 1.

Johnny patented his design for Raggedy Ann. A patent means that no one can steal the design. This patent proved that Johnny owned it.

Raggedy Ann

To fight his sadness over his daughter's death, Johnny began a new project in 1915. He created a series about some silly ducks named Quacky Doodles, Danny Doodles, and Little Doodles. He **patented** (PAT-en-ted) his drawings of the ducks. This meant that he had proof he owned them. The Quacky Doodles drawings were turned into toys. Later, the ducks would appear in silent **animated** (a-neh-MAY-ted) films.

At the same time that he'd **patented** the Quacky Doodles designs, Johnny also patented the design for Raggedy Ann. He and other family members hand-sewed several more copies of the doll. Rag dolls were not new.

Children had been playing with them since the time of ancient Egypt and the pyramids (PEER-uh-mids). Johnny wanted Raggedy Ann to become a popular toy.

By 1917, Johnny was hard at work writing stories about Raggedy Ann. Soon he had enough stories to make a book. In 1918, *Raggedy Ann Stories* was published.

Johnny decided that Raggedy Ann needed a brother. In 1920, Raggedy Andy appeared in

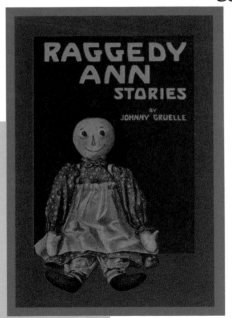

Johnny started writing the Raggedy Ann stories in the early 1900s. This particular Raggedy Ann book was published in 1918.

Johnny decided to give Raggedy Ann a brother and named him Raggedy Andy. In 1920 Raggedy Andy started to appear in his stories also.

Raggedy Andy Stories. Both the books and the dolls made from his designs became very popular. More stories about the sister and brother rag dolls were published every year. There were Raggedy Ann and Andy **animated** films, greeting cards, dishes, and place mats. Even though Johnny wrote many other books, Raggedy Ann and Andy are still the most popular characters he ever created.

There's an old tale about Raggedy Ann. It claims that she has a heart made out of candy. In Raggedy Ann Stories, Johnny did write that she had a candy heart. Did the early Raggedy Ann dolls have candy hearts? Some people think so, but nobody can prove that they did. Even so, it's a sweet story.

Here are the rag doll brother and sister. The top photo is of some of the original dolls made back in the early 1900s by the Volland Company. The bottom photo is of the more modern Raggedy Ann and Andy dolls made by the Applause Company.

Raggedy Ann and Andy Live On

Johnny and Myrtle lived happily together for many years. They had two healthy sons, Worth and Richard, and watched them grow up into fine young men. They moved to Florida to enjoy the warm weather. They had earned enough money from the Raggedy Ann and Andy books and dolls to let them live comfortably.

Then Johnny was diagnosed (DYE-ug-NOHSED) with heart disease. As the years passed, he grew weaker and thinner. On January 10, 1938, he died.

Raggedy Ann and Andy lived on. Myrtle watched over the business for her sons. Johnny's brother, Justin, and his son, Worth,

Myrtle watches her baby son, Worth. She looks amused. Worth must have just figured out how to crawl.

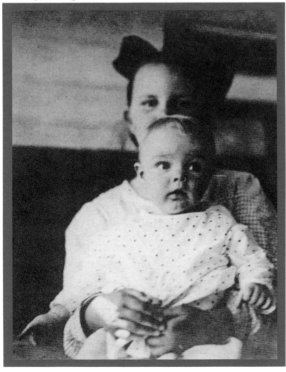

Marcella holds her baby brother on her lap. Her face is almost hidden by him. Marcella was probably 11 years old at the time of this photo.

illustrated several Raggedy Ann books to carry on the tradition (tra-DIH-shun). Myrtle died in 1968. Worth and his brother Richard are also **deceased** (dih-SEASED). Richard's widow, Ruth, is alive and helps oversee Raggedy activities.

Today, the dolls and their adventures can be found in bookstores and on toy store shelves. The earlier dolls, dishes, and cards are eagerly sought by **collectors**. There is also the Johnny Gruelle Raggedy Ann & Andy Museum in Arcola, Illinois. The museum is founded and run by Tom and Joni (JOAN-ee) Gruelle Wannamaker. Joni is Johnny's first grandchild and his namesake.

But the best part about the Raggedy Ann and Andy characters is the man who created them. Johnny is still known as a kind and gentle man. There is a love of good deeds in the books, but that doesn't make them dull reading. They are also very funny and original fantasies (FAN-tuh-sees). Maybe that is why they are still so very popular, over eighty-five years after they were first created. Raggedy Ann and Andy are fun for both children and adults.

Johnny sits with an audience of dolls. He has a Raggedy Andy doll on his knee. It looks like he is pretending to read to the dolls.

Johnny even had a Raggedy Ann and Andy logo painted on the side of his van. He looks amused about the idea.

Johnny was born in Arcola, Illinois. The town put up this monument in his honor. They are proud of him and his many children's books.

In 2002 Raggedy Ann was inducted into the National Toy Hall of Fame. This is the best award a toy can receive. Raggedy Ann wears the news embroidered on her apron. Next to her is an Arcola doll. She's another version of Raggedy Ann made for the town of Arcola. Both dolls were designed by members of the Raggedy Ann and Andy Museum.

1913 *Mr. Twee Deedle*

1918 *Raggedy Ann Stories*

1920 *Raggedy Andy Stories: Introducing the Little Rag Brother of Raggedy Ann*

1924 *Raggedy Ann and Andy and the Camel with the Wrinkled Knees; Raggedy Ann's Number Book*

1925 *Raggedy Ann's Wishing Pebble; Raggedy Ann's Alphabet Book*

1926 *Beloved Belindy; The Paper Dragon*

1927 *Wooden Willie*

1928 *Raggedy Ann's Magical Wishes*

1929 *Marcella: A Raggedy Ann Story*

1930 *Raggedy Ann in the Deep Deep Woods; Raggedy Ann's Sunny Songs*

1931 *Raggedy Ann in Cookie Land*

1932 *Raggedy Ann's Lucky Pennies*

1935 *Raggedy Ann and the Left-Handed Safety Pin; Raggedy Ann Cut-Out Paper Doll; Raggedy Ann in the Golden Meadow*

1937 *Raggedy Ann's Joyful Songs; Raggedy Ann and Maizie Moocow*

—Following Johnny's death in 1938, a lot more books have been published and continue to be published.

1880 Johnny Gruelle is born on December 24 in Arcola, Illinois.

1901 Johnny marries Myrtle Swann.

1910 Johnny wins the *New York Herald*'s cartooning contest and starts the *Mr. Twee Deedle* comic strip. Johnny and Myrtle move to Connecticut.

1913 Johnny's first book, *Mr. Twee Deedle,* is published.

1915 Johnny's daughter, Marcella, dies. Johnny creates the Quacky Doodles books and toys. Raggedy Ann is patented.

1918 *Raggedy Ann Stories* is published.

1920 *Raggedy Andy Stories* is published.

1938 Johnny dies on January 10 in Miami Springs, Florida.

1968 Myrtle dies.

1999 The Raggedy Ann and Andy Museum opens in Arcola, Illinois, in May.

2002 Raggedy Ann was inducted into the National Toy Hall of Fame.

2005 Raggedy's Ann's 90th birthday.

animated film (a-neh-MAY-ted)—drawn cartoon characters that move.

cartoon (KAR-toon)—a funny drawing, often with a few words.

cartoonist (KAR-too-nist)—someone who creates cartoons.

collectors (KAH-lekt-ter)—people who collect certain items, such as Raggedy Ann dolls.

comic strip (KAH-mik strip)—a series of drawings in a row that tell a story or part of a story.

continuing comic strip (KUN-tin-you-ing KAH-mik strip)—a comic strip that is carried by a newspaper or magazine for many issues.

deceased (dih-seased)—died.

patent (pah-TENT)—legal proof that a person owns the design of something.

pseudonym (SUE-duh-nim)—a made up name.

vaccination (vak-seh-NAY-shun)—medicine put into the body, usually through a needle, to prevent disease.

valvular (val-VU-ler)—a vein to the heart that affects the flow of bodily fluids.

Commire, Anne. *Something About the Author,* vol. 35. Detroit: Gale Research, 1964.

Garrison, Susan Ann. *The Raggedy Ann and Andy Family Album.* West Chester, Pennsylvania: Schiffer Publishing, 1989.

Gruelle, Johnny. *The Raggedy Ann Stories: The Very First Raggedy Ann Stories.* New York: Derrydale, 1994.

_____. *Raggedy Andy Stories: Introducing the Little Rag Brother of Raggedy Ann.* New York: Simon & Schuster (reprint), 1993.

_____. *Raggedy Ann Stories.* New York: Simon & Schuster (reprint), 1993.

_____. *Original Adventures of Raggedy Ann.* New York: Random House, 1988.

_____. *How Raggedy Ann Got Her Heart.* New York: Aladdin, 2001.

Hall, Patricia. *Raggedy Ann and More: Johnny Gruelle's Dolls and Merchandise.* Gretna, Louisiana: Pelican Publishing Company, 2000.

Web Sites
The Johnny Gruelle Raggedy Ann & Andy Museum
http://www.raggedyann-museum.org/
The Simon & Schuster page about Johnny Gruelle
http://www.simonsays.com/content/
content.cfm?sid=686&pid=351795

INDEX

Gruelle, Alice (mother) 9

Gruelle, Johnny

   Becomes assistant
illustrator,
*Indianapolis
Star* 10

   Becomes sports
cartoonist, *The
Cleveland Press* 10

   Birth 9

   Birth of daughter,
Marcella 10

   Birth of sons, Worth
and Richard 23

   Creates Mr. Twee
Deedle 13, 14

   Creates Raggedy
Ann 14

   Creates Quacky
Doodles 19

   Death of
Marcella 16, 19

   Death of Myrtle 25

   Death of sons, Worth
and Richard 25

   Dies of heart
disease 23

   Marries Myrtle
Swann 10

   Patents Raggedy Ann
and Quacky
Doodles 18, 29

   Wins *New York Herald*
cartoon contest 7,
13

Gruelle, Justin 5, 9, 25

Gruelle, Prudence 9

Gruelle, Richard
(father) 9

Gruelle, Richard (son)
23, 25

Gruelle Wannamaker,
Tom and Joni 25

Gruelle, Worth 23–25

Johnny Gruelle Raggedy
Ann and Andy
Musuem 25, 27

National Toy Hall of
Fame 27

Raggedy Andy Stories is
published 21

Raggedy Ann Stories is
published 21

Volland Company 22